This book belongs to:

_____

The Adventures of Little Leroy

The Legacy of Martin Luther King, Jr.

Pamela Jarmon Wade

Illustrations by Brandon Coleman

AuthorHouse™
1663 Liberty Drive
Bloomington, IN 47403
www.authorhouse.com
Phone: 1-800-839-8640

Published by AuthorHouse 12/22/2011

ISBN: 978-1-4685-2567-0 (sc)

Library of Congress Control Number: 2011962665

Any people depicted in stock imagery provided by Thinkstock are models,
and such images are being used for illustrative purposes only.
Certain stock imagery © Thinkstock. Author Headshot by Kerry Beyer

This book is printed on acid-free paper.

authorHOUSE®

MY INSPIRATION-

This book is dedicated in memory of: Mable Corprew Jarmon, Leroy Jarmon Sr., Baby Leroy Jr., and the legacy of Dr. Martin Luther King Jr.

MY MOTIVATION-

I also dedicate this book to Anthony Bowman, Cuba & India McLean, Eileen & Gisselle Garcia, Abel Hurtado, and my future grandchildren. As you grow up, please remember that one hundred years from now it will not matter what your bank balance was, the sort of house you lived in, or the kind of car you drove...but it will always matter that the USA is a better place for everyone because of Dr. Martin Luther King, Jr.

One day, Little Leroy's Dad brought home a DVD. It was a magical movie about Martin Luther King, Jr. He knew that it was time that he formally introduce Little Leroy to Martin Luther King, Jr. It was also time to plan a family vacation, so he decided to make this an educational family vacation. "Hi Dad, I'm glad you are home from work!" exclaimed Little Leroy as he and his beloved dog Spot happily ran to greet him. Spot anxiously wagged his tail knowing that he would soon be lavished with pats on the head and belly rubs. "Hi Son, so am I. I have something for you."

"Thanks, Dad!" said Little Leroy. Little Leroy looked at the cover of the DVD and saw two boys that were about his age. He saw a skateboard and clock. He also saw Martin Luther King, Jr. whom he had informally heard about. "Son, Dr. King is an icon who died for his belief that all people are equal, regardless of race, creed, or color. He used non-violent marches to fight for civil rights for himself, his children, us, and the world. Your mother and I would like for us to attend the Monument Dedication in Washington, D.C. as part of our vacation this year. We will witness a historic event for the dedication of The Martin Luther King, Jr. National Memorial. This is the first memorial on the National Mall for a person of color. It's the first for a non-president and man of peace."

"Wow Dad...YES! I will have an awesome story to share with my friends, classmates, and teachers." gleamed Little Leroy. "Son the sharing of you witnessing such a historic event should be recounted for a lifetime. It will extend beyond friends to family, strangers, journalist, and even your grandchildren one day."

"Now I want you to meet Dr. King." said his dad. His dad played the DVD so that Little Leroy could get acquainted with the legacy of Martin Luther King, Jr. before attending the upcoming dedication. Little Leroy watched in awe. "Unity! Unity! Unity!" Little Leroy said at the ending. "Yes! Son you got it. Martin Luther King, Jr. leaves a legacy of justice, democracy, hope, love, and unity. The election of President Barack Obama as the first black president fulfills a portion of Dr. King's dream. This year we will collect an unforgettable experience instead of just souvenirs when we visit the MLK Memorial Monument. We can go back again and again. When you grow up and start a family, please take your family too."

"As far as we have come in The United States of America, there is still room for growth. Parents and schools should not limit Black History to 28 days...it should be 365 days. There is so much Black History that a lot of schools never educate and inform the students about." his mother sternly said.

12

"Can you provide us with an example of something that you learned from the DVD?" asked his dad. "Yes." Little Leroy said as he grabbed his magician's hat and thinking about his Black, Hispanic, and White friends. He dropped a handful of marbles into the hat. He waved his hand, then Little Leroy pulled out a black marble...then he pulled out a white marble...then he pulled out a brown marble. Little Leroy told his dad, "I learned that all people are equal... black, white, and brown." "That's true son." said his dad. "It does not matter what color the marbles are. They are all equal. They are all marbles, just like people." said his dad. "That's love and unity!" said Little Leroy.

There was a knock at the door. It was James Garcia and Clyde Perry... his friends. James and Clyde had a special knock which always let Little Leroy know it was his best buds. As Little Leroy's mom went to answer the door, the conversation continued.

"Son, no matter what some improperly informed person may tell you about Dr. King...always remember that Dr. King left a wealth of resources behind. You can read his books and listen to his speeches for yourself, so that you will know firsthand, "THE KING PHILOSOPHY". He paved the way for you to be friends with all races and nationalities.

The boys went to Little Leroy's room for a game of marbles. As his mother and father looked at the game...Little Leroy said, "Thanks to Martin we can be together to eat, work, pray, and play no matter what color we are. My dad got me a DVD that tells all about Dr. Martin Luther King. He was a great black man that cared about all of us."

Then Little Leroy looked at his parents and asked, "Can you tell James and Clyde's parents about the DVD?"

"Yes son, I'm so happy that you want to share what you learned. I will call their parents and invite them all over to watch and discuss the DVD this weekend. Maybe we can plan a group vacation next year to the MLK Center for Nonviolent Social Change in Atlanta, Georgia. Let's keep Dr. Martin Luther King's dream alive."

Pamela on the King Center Campus admiring the historic Ebenezer Baptist Church

(historic sign not in this photo).

Pamela in front of mounted photo of Dr. King's casket on a farm wagon drawn by mules. The wagon is on display at The King Center, which was established by Mrs. Coretta Scott King (Atlanta, Georgia).

Pamela and Layle McKelvey in front of Dr. King's Crypt which is located on The King Center Campus. Since this photo was taken, the Crypt has been rebuilt to also hold the remains of Mrs. Coretta Scott King.

Pamela at the birth home of Martin Luther King, Jr. on Auburn Avenue

(Atlanta, Georgia).

Dr. King Quick Query

01. Where was Dr. King born?

02. What month do we celebrate the National King Holiday?

03. Where did Dr. King deliver his famous, "I Have a Dream" speech?

04. When was Dr. King assassinated?

05. Did Dr. King support striking sanitation workers in Memphis?

06. What is the title of Dr. King's final speech?

07. Who was Dr. King married to?

08. How many children did Dr. King have?

09. Whose nonviolent strategy for social change did Dr. King study?

10. Did Dr. King have a comedic side in private?

11. Where is the King Monument?

12. Where is the King Center?

13. Where is Dr. King's crypt?

14. What church did Dr. King co-pastor?

15. Was Dr. King's name at birth Michael King?

16. Was Dr. King a Morehouse College Alumnus?

17. Dr. King's Doctoral studies were at Boston University's School of Theology.

Dr. King Quick Query Answers

01. Atlanta, GA

02. January

03. On the steps of the Lincoln Memorial

04. April 4, 1968

05. Yes

06. "I've Been to the Mountaintop"

07. Coretta Scott King

08. Four

09. Mahatma Gandhi

10. Yes

11. Washington, D.C.

12. Atlanta, GA

13. Atlanta, GA

14. Ebenezer Baptist Church

15. True/Yes

16. True/Yes

17. True/Yes

Dear Parents, Teachers, Librarians:

First, I thank you for purchasing this book. I am so happy that my character, Little Leroy, went from a dream to reality. This character has played with me for years and is named after my brother who was born and died in Norfolk, Virginia ten years before my birth. Upon my mother's death in 1978, I received my brother's birth certificate. Upon my father's death in 2002, I received my brother's hospital card, a receipt from a trip to the emergency room at Norfolk County Hospital, and a letter that my dad wrote to my mother detailing how proud he was to have had a son and how deeply the loss of Leroy Jr. cut into his heart. As I read the letter I could see my father on the military base writing home to his grieving wife and wishing that he could have stayed with her longer...but his obligation to return to the Army base was a must. My mom, dad, and brother are my angels and they cheer me on to follow my dreams...so that is why this book is dedicated to their memory.

My parents instilled in me a deep sense of respect for Dr. Martin Luther King, Jr. and that inspired me to write this book. I supported "Build the Dream" with a couple of donations to the Washington DC Martin Luther King, Jr. National Memorial Project Foundation which helped make a memorial on the National Mall become a reality. If you want to honor Dr. King and his vision for America, you can still donate by going to www.mlkmemorial.org or by texting MLK to 20222. All contributions are tax deductible.

The Martin Luther King Jr. Center for Nonviolent Social Change is also known as The King Center and was established by Mrs. Coretta Scott King. It is located in Atlanta, Georgia. Donations are accepted to assist with the mission to educate the world about Dr. King's teachings. For more information on donating to The King Center, email information@thekingcenter.org.

Printed in the United States
by Baker & Taylor Publisher Services